For, My Phenomenal Grandmothers:

The late, beautiful and talented, Roberta Holman Newell

&

The radiant and gifted, Melva Kelly Brinkley

Thank You

Table of Contents

Preface 7

Why I Returned Natural 9

New Hair, Who Dis? 17

Don't Stereotype My Hair Type 23

Fro Envy 29

Protect What God Gave You 39

My Hair Will Not Be My Idol 43

Shrinkage is Not the Devil 47

Wash Day is Like Sunday Service For Hair 51

When Deep Conditioning Conditions
Your Soul 57

Hi, My Name is Janay and I am a Recovering
Product Junkie 63

How I Got Punished With Heat Damage 69

Trims are Necessary 77

Why I Have a Love-Hate Relationship With YouTube Hair Tutorials 81

Chicks With the Kinks Still Get the Winks...... 87

You are Your Hair.. 97

God, Do You Like My Fro?................................. 103

About the Author... 111

Preface

I am so grateful and honored to be physically, mentally and spiritually able to walk in my purpose. Each day that the Lord has granted me, I have tried my best to utilize my gifts so that I do not waste the opportunity of being blessed with life. It is a privilege to be willing and able, to be used by the Holy Spirit to glorify God. He has given me the ability to be creative and relevant, all while being myself. I am blessed to be a blessing to others. I praise His Holy Name for that.

How can hair teach someone about faith? The Lord has clearly shown me that He is able to do any and everything if you allow Him. I have learned that there is no limit to how awesome God can be when we do not place Him in a box. I hope that as you read, you will laugh and find some humor in life. I pray that as you read, you feel inspired and motivated to be better through Christ. I pray that the Lord speaks to you in an intimate way, and that you know that it is Him talking. I pray that my transparency allows others to be honest and open about their faults, flaws and failures, while still reminding them to see the grace of God throughout their growth. I pray that this book allows others to appreciate the natural beauty that we were all born with through something as simple as our hair. I pray that this book restores people's self-confidence and Christ-confidence. Most importantly, I pray that this book will allow us all to see how God is in every single thing that we do; He tactfully grabs our attention so that He can use us for His glory. In Jesus' Mighty and Holy Name, I pray all these things come to fruition.

Why I Returned Natural

I wish I had something deep and inspiring to share with you about why I decided to go natural, but I don't. To be transparent, the more I looked in the mirror to examine my hair, which then was chemically treated, the more I noticed how frail, brittle, thin and short my strands were becoming. It bothered me how my hair, once long and durable, became my worst nightmare in a blink of an eye. I thought I was doing a decent job with my maintenance of it (considering that I was twelve hours away from home for college) away from my mother's help. She was no longer doing my hair or scheduling my hair appointments and I was proud to be promoted to do it myself. But clearly, I didn't know how much responsibility and consistency came with this new promotion. It took my mother over ten years of late-night braiding sessions, long hours of hot oil treatments and regular strategic touch-up appointments to grow my hair to mid-back. This all took place while I participated in competitive sports, which required extra attention on my hair due to my constant sweating. When I decided that I wanted to grow out my natural hair, all I wanted was that same "swingage" (when your hair is so long and soft that it swings effortlessly with motion) that I took for granted back in 2009 with my once chemically treated hair. With the rise in popularity of natural hair, I noticed the remarkable hair growth from naturalistas all across the globe. I wanted "in" on the black sister secret of growing longer hair. Just for the record, I'm only referring to returning to my natural state of hair as "going natural" because of the phrase's popularity, which is widely used in the curly hair community. I believe that with natural hair, we return to our natural state. Here is my best explanation of what *returning natural* is:

> *To return natural, you have to rid yourself of all texture-altering chemicals, which were placed in your hair. It was once very popular to relax or perm black women's hair in order for it to be straighter, and thus more manageable. A perm, also known as the "Creamy Crack" or "Crème de la Crème," includes lye, a substance that burns your scalp like Satan's spit, if kept in*

too long. You can restore your chemically-processed hair to its original state by doing one of two things: slowly trimming the ends of your chemically treated hair as the "new growth" develops—the kinky/curly hair growing from your roots that you'd once smother with gel before your next touch-up appointment—or cutting all of your chemically treated hair off, leaving just your new growth, aka "the big chop." Once all of the chemically treated hair is cut off, either by patiently waiting for it to grow out or chopping it all off at once, you are officially "natural."

The "transition method," cutting off the permed hair little by little, was certainly my preferred method of going natural. The "big chop" simply wouldn't suit this big head that God has blessed me with. That is my story, and I'm sticking to it. My plan was to first grow out every inch of chemically-treated hair, and once it reached a certain length, I was going to treat my hair with the *Crème de la Crème* for a long awaited reunion. I was assured that this would be the best way to achieve healthy, long hair again.

During my transition to natural hair, what I learned completely changed my perspective on what the natural life was about. Transitioning is one of the most ugly, difficult and frustrating periods of a soon-to-be natural girl's life. As my natural hair grew out, I questioned my entire standards of beauty. I looked in the mirror plenty of times and asked myself, "Do I still look beautiful?" Transitioning takes patience, perseverance, discipline and hope. After I finally cut off all of my chemically treated hair and I was comfortable with my new natural hair, it was *then* that I realized that transitioning was essential for me to appreciate the process.

Where your new growth and your old processed hair meet is the point on your strands that you are supposed to cut. At this point, you can clearly see the drastic difference in texture of your hair. At this point, your curly-kinky strands battle it out to take sole ownership of your head. This point of division is where your hair gets tangled, matted and knotted. Fighting to keep hold of my hair for length, I battled with self-made knots, I ripped out chunks of my hair and I broke two combs. I created a mess in the middle of my scalp with uneven strand lengths, which was a result of me impatiently foregoing a gentle detangling process and getting scissor-happy instead. I wanted to hold onto long length so badly because I wasn't fully comfortable with wearing the length of my new growth yet.

As I tried to make something of my two different textures, others began to notice that I was on a natural hair journey. I got weird looks and disapproving comments like, "Oh girl, I just couldn't go natural and have my nappy head all out, I need a perm!" or "Umm, what's going on with your hair? When are you going to get it done?" My favorite encounter was when I would talk to someone and notice their eyes slowly wander off from my eyes to my hairline and then right back to my eyes, *as if they didn't just judge my entire life in a matter of seconds.* I would love to tell you that I was so rooted back then that I ignored all the comments and kept it moving. But I can't. The comments bothered me because I didn't see the beauty in my own transition to be secure enough to block out everyone else. Due to my lack of confidence and patience, I decided to cover the mess I made with different styles to make transitioning smoother. I guess it worked. I tried my best to "blend in" with the evolving weave trends to disguise my ugly transition.

Finally, after almost a year of braids, Senegalese Twists, sew-in weaves, Remy Virgin synthetic hair, U-Part wigs and flexi rod curl extension clip-ins, I was officially natural! My stylist at the time had snipped off the last inch of my permed hair, leaving me with my awaited thick and unruly hair! I was so excited to be natural, and I had no clue as to what I was doing. All I knew was that it felt like a big weight had been lifted off my shoulders, and I genuinely felt like myself.

Reminiscing on my transitioning journey, returning natural was symbolic to me, and quite eerily synchronized with the timing of my rededication to Christ. Just as I returned back to my natural state of hair, I returned back to my commitment to live for Christ. At first, I thought I was just rededicating my life back to Jesus because I knew I needed a change in lifestyle; but it was more than that. I didn't like the person looking back at me in the mirror. I despised that she wasn't growing. I couldn't stand to watch her succumb to the pressures of the world. She was losing her identity. I had done things my way and failed; and the deteriorating changes were starting to show. Despite the example my mother and others set for me of praying, attending church regularly and living righteously, I failed to pay close attention to the reason behind their dedication to Christ. I had to find out who Jesus was on my own. I had to rid myself of all the "chemicals" in my life that stunted my growth and burned me when they lingered too long. The Bible told me in Proverbs 22:6, "Train up a child in the way he should go, And when he is old he will not depart from it." I now know that I was always destined to return, but it was just my decision to make in God's time. The decision to return would either be by slowly transitioning from my old way of living, to living for Christ, or it would require me to completely and immediately leave the world behind to live boldly for Christ. It didn't matter which way I chose, but it mattered that I made the choice.

Reflecting back on everything, I wish I had the audacity to do a big chop, spiritually and naturally. When you big chop, you see immediate results, you immediately start your journey and you immediately begin growing. I actually wish I never chemically-altered my hair or my life. I wish that I never strayed away from His presence. I wish I could tell my younger self to not delay what God had in store for me by making a slow spiritual transition. Even so, transitioning, although ugly and painful, was worth it. When I finally saw the growth, I was pleased. The more my hair grew, the more I progressed; the more change I saw in myself, the easier it was for me to eliminate toxicity from my life. Slowly but surely, I realized who I was meant to be and what I was created for.

People didn't recognize me anymore. They hated this new look and wanted the old me back. "Too late, this is the new me now," I repeated to myself as I regained lost confidence. Even when I tried my best to hide my transition in order to look like the world, my new growth would eventually show. I couldn't hide who I was called to be. I was gaining the courage and strength to be bold in who God made me. He had so much in store for me and I didn't even realize it. I had my reasons for returning natural, but His purpose through it was far greater than anything I could have ever planned. Despite myself, the Lord began manifesting His purpose in my life.

New Hair, Who Dis?

After I finally got rid of my dead ends, I embraced being a new naturalista. I experienced the world in a refreshing way. I learned very quickly that with a new life came new habits and a new lifestyle. Just as I rededicated my life to Christ and I had returned back to my natural hair, things would be different than what I was used to.

There were many things that I had to change and let go of, for my new journey. No more sleeping at night without a scarf, no more shampoos with stripping sulfates or drying alcohol, no more harsh blow-drying or damaging flat-ironing. I had to learn how to apply leave-in conditioner in my hair periodically throughout the week for moisture; I had to go to stylists who specialize in natural hair care; I had to learn how to separate my hair at night into mini pineapples (curly-haired ponytails) so my hair wouldn't matte or tangle; I had to learn the discipline to leave the flat iron alone for months at a time; I had to learn how to sleep with a bonnet or satin pillow case; I had to learn how to drink more water and eat a healthier diet and I also had to learn to shop at specialty stores for natural hair. Everything I did would either nourish my hair or damage it. If any particular product or method impeded my hair growth or reversed my efforts, it had to go. I was conforming to a new hair regimen, which meant that I had to establish a new lifestyle.

Conviction laid heavy on me during my transition. I knew the moment I decided to return natural and the moment I rededicated my life to Christ that there had to be a difference in my actions, 2 Corinthians 5:17 says, "Therefore, if anyone is in Christ, he is a new creation; old things have passed away; behold, all things have become new." How could I call myself a Christian while continuing to look like the world, full of breakage and split ends? How could I call myself a true natural when I neglected even the basics for healthy growth? 1 Peter 2:9 (KJV) reads, "But ye are a chosen generation, a royal priesthood, an holy nation, a peculiar people; that ye should shew forth the praises of him who hath called you out of darkness into his marvelous light." If we are truly in Christ, then we are not of this world; we walk differently, we talk differently and we act differently. We are peculiar. Naturals act differently and are easily recognizable because of how unique and peculiar we are compared to the rest of society. Naturals, just like Christians, are not modeled after society. When society doesn't accept our ways, we embrace our uniqueness.

My lifestyle had to change; everything had to go. I had to humble myself and change for the better (Romans 2:8). No more drinking alcohol of any kind (1 Peter 5:8; Proverbs 20:1), no more going to clubs (1 Thessalonians 5:22), no more dressing provocatively to invite lustful attention to myself (Romans 14:13), no more sex or sexual activities outside of marriage (fornication; 1 Corinthians 6:18; 1 Thessalonians 4:3), no more foul language (Ephesians 4:29), no more listening to music with messages that promote sexual deviancy, promiscuity, violence, blasphemy, drugs and alcohol (Galatians 5:19-21), no more agreeing or flirting with the world's values in public and then consummating with God's values in private (James 1:8), and no more denying of my true identity in Christ (Romans 8:16-17). This was just the beginning.

I had to learn how to read and study the Bible. I had to learn to pray consistently. I prayed that I would both receive and desire the conviction and correction of the Holy Spirit; my carnal desires and human understanding had to go. Proverbs 3:5-6 reminded me to "Trust in the Lord with all your heart, and lean not on your own understanding; In all your ways acknowledge Him, and He shall direct your paths." I had to learn how to pray effectively in the Name of Jesus. I had to learn how to get serious about my attendance at church and then continue to carry the presence of God with me throughout the week. I had to learn meekness—that not everything deserves a smart response. I learned to be quiet and let God vindicate me. I had to learn the true meaning of joy despite my circumstances; the joy that He has given me can never be taken away. I had to learn that the love story I was searching for in a romantic relationship was found in Jesus dying on the cross for me years ago. I had to learn how to be confident in spreading the truth of the gospel, without my own two-cents. I had to learn how to love with no conditions and forgive like I'd never been hurt before. 1 Corinthians 13:11 says, "When I was a child, I spoke as a child, I understood as a child, I thought as a child; but when I became a man, I put away childish things." When I became a woman in Christ, all of the childish things of my past had to go—mindset included.

When I returned natural, all of the hair care habits that I once knew also had to change. As you return natural, you face opposition from those who don't understand; in the same way, when you lay down your life for Christ, you will face opposition from those who don't understand. I had to come to the awareness that I would rather please God than myself, my family, my boyfriend, my friends or anyone else. Just as I won't let anything jeopardize my hair health, I won't let anyone jeopardize my eternity in Heaven, either. So believe it when I say, "New Hair, Who Dis?"

Don't Stereotype My Hair Type

Dear Mr. Andre Walker,

Don't take this to heart, but I just wanted to let you know that I strongly dislike hair typing. I may sound brash but this is honest—it just doesn't work for me. I don't fit in one singular category of your hair typing system and over the years, guess what? My hair type has changed! So what's the use? "4A, 4B, 4C"... hair typing makes me sound like the model of a car! The biggest reason why I don't like hair typing is because hair companies have piggy-backed off your system to sell me on a formula specifically tailored to "4B/4C girls only," and guess what? It didn't work!

P.S. I haven't tried your products yet, but I mean, feel free to slide some free samples over here if you want.

Sincerely,
Ms. Brinkley

As you can see, I do not like hair typing. This is nothing against Mr. Andre Walker. It just doesn't work for me. I get frustrated with all of the division that comes with the hair typing system, especially when it was first introduced. As a naïve and new member of the natural hair community, I thought being natural was everyone having thick, curly and luscious hair. I understood that everyone had different hair shapes, sizes and textures, but when it was broken down into the smallest discrepancies such as "curly-coily" or "ziggy-kinky," I got overwhelmed. Then, it didn't help that the natural hair community, which is largely comprised of the African American female population, had allowed this hair typing system to creep in and ignite the spark of the pretty prejudice—solely basing beauty on vain characteristics such as hair, weight and/or skin tone. I was relieved by unity amongst African American women through hair, only to again see a community divided by the same false beauty standards that separated us in the beginning. It was a re-run of Spike Lee's *School Daze* movie, seeing the JiggaBoos combat the WannaBe's, the light-skinned-mixed-chick's coils versus the mocha-melanin-girl's kinks. It was the resurrection of the house slave versus the field negro....and where did I fit into this vain division, being light-skinned with kinky, coily hair? "It's okay to go natural as long as you have big, loose curls that hang past your shoulders," is what the ignorant bystanders were supporting based on what they "liked" and "shared" on social media. I cringed at the blatant bias in the disproportionate amount of heart emojis under a lighter-skinned child's picture with "good hair" in proportion to a darker-skinned child's picture with afro-puffs.

I would like to stop here to rant about the foolishness of those obsessing over having lighter-skinned children, thinking they are going to be more attractive than darker-skinned children. We are all made in the image of God and He never told us that a certain skin tone is valued higher than another. Being mixed or light-skinned doesn't make you superior or more beautiful, and being darker-skinned doesn't validate that you are more "black" and therefore worth being accepted into African or African American culture. If you have lighter skin, you shouldn't have to validate your "blackness" and if you have darker skin, you shouldn't feel inadequate in beauty. Let's push back on these superficial divisions and instead encourage unity through Christ. We have all been created and colored in different shades and hues, and that's beautiful. Let's all be thankful for being uniquely created, as God's creations are marvelous in the eyes of the Lord. That is something to celebrate!

I believe that we, as the natural hair community, have improved in this matter. We may have come to a peaceful celebration and acceptance of all "hair types," but we can always do better.

Just like the natural hair community, we too as Christians fall under the same pressures to classify and separate each other based on denominations. Most denominations serve one God, have accepted Jesus Christ as their Lord and Savior, acknowledge the Holy Spirit and live by the principles and standards of the Holy Bible. So why do we have such separation? 1 Corinthians 12:12-14 reminds us, "For as the body is one and has many members, but all the members of that one body, being many, are one body, so also is Christ. For by one Spirit we were all baptized into one body, whether Jews or Greeks, whether slaves or free, and have all been made to drink into one Spirit." It doesn't matter how different we think we are in our personal principles or preference of worship. God sees us all as one in Christ, and if we're one in Christ, we should be unified. Religious leaders from our past have dissected certain scriptures from God's Word and, with no regard to the Holy Spirit, claimed their denomination as the best practice to serve our unbiased God. We have fallen into this system by adopting a "type" we think we fit into and based on the description of what each denomination stands for, and we may frown upon others who choose a different one. I desire and pray to see churches of Jesus Christ, as a whole, do better. I believe that Pentecostal churches, Baptist churches, Methodist churches, Holiness churches, and many others, would be *even more* effective in their communities and the lives of believers, if they broke down all of their man-made barriers—particularly pride. It would break my heart if we let the religious spirit choke out and suffocate the beautiful relationship that God has formed with us.

Moral of the story: I don't like hair typing.

Fro Envy

Okay—transparent moment. I follow a lot of natural hair pages and I see a lot of gorgeous natural hair on my feed. I sometimes find myself scrolling through Instagram, and I will catch myself gawking over every thick, full, curly mane that I lay eyes upon. Then, I will often find someone that has the best, and I mean *the best*, twist-out-definition-to-length ratio that I've ever seen. I'll click on her name and scroll through her profile, and then I'll go ahead and ask the usual natural hair resume questions and thoughts to myself:

> *"Okay, before I get all fascinated, is this even all her hair? Yeah, it is, okay she's legit. How did she get that definition? What did she do, leave her twist in for three days? What products does she use? Oh, she must have money because I am not spending that much on those products. But wait, I do the same twisting method, why doesn't my hair*

turn out like that? How long has she been natural?"

As I scroll through every single picture that showcases her Wash Day routine and styling method, I proceed to hit the follow button. After I have finished my snooping and evaluation, I've officially decided that Instagram User @Diva_BigChop_7536 is my new model for **#HairGoals**. All of her pictures and video clips showcase that her hair is soft, bouncy and full while her life appears to be carefree and exciting. In my mind, I'm thinking, "*Girl, if I knew you in real life, we would be **#Curlfriends**.*" Before I click the back arrow, I read something that makes me disappointed with myself and @Diva_BigChop_7536. Her profile description reads that she has only been natural for 7 months.

"How in the world did she big chop and her hair has grown longer than mine in 7 months?! Really, God? Really?! I have been natural for three years now, taking hair growing pills, drinking water, exercising, getting regular trims, and I am still sitting here with the same length since 2014!"

Maybe like myself, you replay your hair care routine and think of reasons why your hair isn't growing and how you can get texture just like hers. You like your hair, but you think her hair is better and you want it. If you're real with yourself and you can identify with this in some way or have had a similar social media experience, you, like many others, and myself, had "Fro Envy."

Fro Envy is when you genuinely admire someone's hair for its thickness, fullness, color, curl pattern, style, maintenance and/or length. But, as much as you are genuinely infatuated with their hair, you feel equally discontent with yours. You're secretly envious of their current state of hair glory and you desire what they have.

Jealousy and envy are often grouped together, yet very different. Merriam-Webster's Dictionary defines jealous as "hostile toward a rival or one believed to enjoy an advantage."

Merriam-Webster defines envy as "painful or resentful awareness of an advantage enjoyed by another joined with a desire to possess the same advantage." To be jealous is to oppose someone for something they have that you feel is a valuable asset, whereas being envious desires to posses that thing of value. While you may celebrate other people's hair via a "like" on social media, you should not covet what they have. Fro Envy will have you obsessing over your hair goals to the point where your natural hair becomes your number-one priority. You begin to believe that achieving hair glory would amount to you reaching another person's level. When I felt like my natural hair journey started to become an obsession due to my own Fro Envy, I had to snap back to reality. I had to constantly repeat to myself that I shouldn't desire anything someone else has, because God gave to me exactly what He wanted me to have. Galatians 6:3-4 says, "For if anyone thinks himself to be something, when he is nothing, he deceives himself. But let each one examine his own work, and then he will have rejoicing in himself alone, and not in another." When I spent too much of my extra time watching hours of YouTube tutorials, I knew that I had to be brought back down to reality to have a "come to Jesus" moment with myself. If I put all of my energy into my hair growth just for it to be as large or as long as someone else's, I was doing it for the wrong reason. I was exposed to my own insecurity and had to hold myself accountable to my shortcomings.

The best motivation can come from seeing others' progress, as long as there is no urgency to compete with that person. If you are motivated to do something and inspired by someone else's journey to make a positive impact, that is a blessing, but don't be consumed by it for the wrong reasons. I have grown to a point in my life where I absolutely love hearing success stories from family, friends and strangers, but I do not envy their success. I don't know what they had to endure to receive their blessing. I can truly say that I do not want what someone else has, because I am convinced, assured and whole-heartedly believe that whatever God has for me is specifically for me. I have an overly confident, even borderline *arrogant* faith that God has tailor-made all that He wants me to have. Once I get it, whatever it is, I will lack absolutely nothing and will be humble in knowing who gave it to me. I am pushed by my family and close friends to do better, but they are not what motivate me. God's love, grace and mercy are what keep me inspired in all that I do. I am motivated and committed to do all things in the spirit of excellence, for His glory and for His Kingdom.

I wasn't always at this point in my relationship with Christ. Much like my natural hair is a journey, my faith is a journey, too. There was a point where I let Fro Envy control my thoughts and emotions. There was a point where I was purely motivated to prove something to people. Thank God that I was delivered from that and set free—never to return again!

People tell me that they want hair like mine and that they're envious of my hair. I don't think that they *truly* understand what they are saying. When people say that, this is what runs through my mind:

> *Wait, you want my hair? You're saying that you're envious of MY hair? Do you know how many days I've cried and pleaded to the Lord for relief because my arms were tired of hanging over my head from detangling? Do you know how long it takes me to wash, deep condition and twist my hair every Wash Day so that I can untwist my hair the next day, only to find that my hair hasn't fully dried yet, and therefore my twists aren't even defined? Do you know how it*

feels when I go to sleep after a good hair day, only to wake with a "Good Times" afro and be expected to "fix" it for a corporate job setting? Do you know how tired I am of wearing a high puff, but I have to, because the middle of my head doesn't want to "play nice" with my kinkier coils located towards the back of my neck, aka my nape naps, aka my "kitchen?" Do you know how nice and curly my hair looks wet, only to get tangled and matted when it dries if I don't detangle? I am convinced that wash-and-go's were just not made for me! Do you know the struggle? Because if you did, I doubt you would be envious of me anymore.

Then I smile at them, suppressing my inner rants, and politely say, "Thank you, but please just embrace what you have."

It's funny because my mother tells me all the time that she loves my hair. She says she wants her hair to be thick and full like mine. My mom has some of the most manageable, soft hair that I have ever touched. With just a drop of water, her curls will pop to life! (My brother's curls behave the same way; the genetics skipped right over me. Thanks, Dad). I enjoy doing my mom's hair because it takes all of thirty minutes to wash, condition and style. She hates her small, tight curls that dry into a bouncy, defined fro. I, on the other hand, absolutely adore her hair. I tell my mom over and over again that she does not want to trade in her thirty-minute Wash Day for my four-hour Wash Day, despite how full it looks. We go back and forth all the time.

This reminds me that you must love what God has given you. Whether it's your hair, your skin, your height, your weight... love all of it. No one knows what others had to go through, what sacrifices they had to make and what the Lord had to rid them of just to make room for their blessing and breakthrough. You can't pray and hope for longer hair if you are not taking care of the hair you already have. You can't plead for more if you're not already a faithful steward over the "few" you may have been given already. Matthew 25:21 says, "His lord said to him, 'Well done, good and faithful servant; you were faithful over a few things, I will make you ruler over many things. Enter into the joy of your lord." There will always be someone or something that may appear to be better than you or what you have. This is called the "compare and distract tactic," which is used by the enemy to draw our attention away from what's important. Instead of focusing on others, we need to focus on ourselves. We compete with no one but ourselves.

I used to spend hours wasting time on social media observing other people's lives through pictures and videos. I found myself caring more about what someone did that day or their accomplishments rather than what I was doing with my own life. I was subconsciously criticizing other people's lives instead of self-assessing my own. I needed to document parts of my life to share with everyone instead of thankfully relishing in the moment, sans phone. Recording your memories is important, but don't let it consume you. Please don't fall into the trap of succumbing to the "compare and distract tactic" on social media. Remember to encourage others to flee this same temptation, too. Others might desire the possessions that you may take for granted! See the beauty in what is yours. Enjoy it. Do not envy the fro, but embrace your own.

Protect What God Gave You

Protective styling is *key*. Protective styling is when you wear low-maintenance, manipulative hairstyles that protect your hair health by not exposing the ends of your hair. Whether you decide to do twists, cornrows, box braids, weaves, wigs or use your own hair, the style you choose is not as important as the style effectively protecting your hair. I have learned that I need protective styles to preserve my growth and lock away my ends from harsh elements. It always makes me laugh when people see me away from my usual fluff twist out and ask if I am still natural, just because I may have a weave or wig that is styled straight. They become even more puzzled when I take the weave out or wig off and have my own hair showing again, sometimes within that same week. If you really don't know me, you might ask questions like, "Hey Janay, did your hair grow?" I laugh to myself and tell them that I am wearing the hair to protect my own. Once I explain this to them, half of the people do not comprehend it. They don't fully understand the process of caring for natural hair. They haven't experienced the strength of being able to manipulate kinky hair into various styles and yet the fragility of taking care of kinky curls for growth and longevity. Whenever I feel like my hair has taken a beating from my constant manipulation, I know then that I need to shelter it under a protective style.

I think every naturalista can agree with the notion that protective styling is only for preservation. We don't *rely* on it. We wear wigs, weaves and extensions for the *health* of our hair—not because we are *ashamed* of our hair. Sometimes we need a break from the daily maintenance and just want to relax without worrying about doing our hair every other day. We don't need the extensions, braids or weaves to make us; they are a tool for our benefit. Everyone needs a little timeout from something. Protective styles are the naturalista's mini vacation from their kinks.

God is so good because, just like the precious, unique hair He placed on our heads, He gave us precious and unique dreams as well. The dreams and visions He has installed in us are of victory, hope and a better future. Just like the

Bible mentions in Jeremiah 29:11, "For I know the thoughts that I think toward you, says the Lord, thoughts of peace and not of evil, to give you a future and a hope." Whatever the Lord has designed for each of us, for His glory, is magnificent and something that will bless us and others greatly.

The vision, the gift and the way to fulfill the purpose for your life have to be protected. Your dream must be shielded from every negative and discouraging element that it will face. Not everyone will be excited for you and your new journey. Some will speak death and defeat into your life while others may gossip about you. Protect what is yours. This also means that not everything that God shares with you needs to be broadcast to the world. Guard your dreams until the appointed time that God says you can reveal what He has for you. Just like how I need to learn to keep my protective styles in longer, I have also learned that not every detail has to be shared with everyone—including family and friends; I need to keep the protection of my dreams and visions "on" longer. God will tell you when it's the right time to let everyone know. Premature announcements are just as harmful as premature movements in life. The longer we leave a protective style in our hair, the greater the chance our hair has of growing without breakage. The longer we work on our plans and properly protect our vision, the faster we will grow.

That being said, you also cannot leave any protective style in for longer than its appointed time. Braids, twists and weaves that stay in longer than 30-50 days without maintenance or care can cause greater damage than growth. The longer you sit on a vision, a gift or a way to fulfill your purpose that God has confirmed and told you to execute, you are causing more damage to yourself than growth. Ecclesiastes 3:1 says, "To everything there is a season, a time for every purpose under heaven." Is it your season of protection, planning, and growth, or is it your season of movement, action, and execution?

My Hair Will Not Be My Idol

There is really nothing *that* special about hair. Hair is just protein bulging out of our scalp, and once it reaches a certain mass of weight, it begins to hang or twirl. We worship it sometimes, like an idol. We bow down and consume ourselves with it. Wearing our hair as a crown, it gives us a superficial and false sense of worth. Hair can be disheartening when we allow it to define our beauty. Hair can even ruin relationships. Society, mothers, husbands or friends tell our sisters that when her hair doesn't look a certain way, she isn't worthy of being called "pretty." They might not say it all the time, but they show it in their actions by frowns of displeasure or smiles of approval. We burden our sisters into feeling shameful for the way her hair appears, so much so that she feels the need to fix what was never broken. God makes no mistakes and He didn't make one when He bestowed her with soft sandy-brown tresses or when He marked her with jet-black kinky roots. They claim that they desire the best interest for her and her hair but never offer a wise alternative for a healthier hair treatment. They couldn't handle the strength and glory that natural hair reveals so they tell her that she can't do the same. They don't understand the maintenance or the history behind the significance of our comb, in a hair pick, so they reject the idea all in one and want her to do the same. They subconsciously place their baggage on her. "Just put a weave in," they say, "A weave will make it better. Just sew this into your braids. It will be easier to manage." They encourage our sister to break that strong bond of cuticles that tell our history with a chemical that does more harm to our spirit than our health. They don't mention the need for true identity in Christ, self-love and assurance. They don't share with her our past wounds from being brainwashed and manipulated into thinking that there was something wrong with us if our hair wasn't straight all the time. They don't ask her to share how their comments might make her feel about herself. They don't realize they push things on her from their own insecurities.

There is a sister, a black woman, who feels like her hair is a disgrace to society, her mother or possibly her husband. Her crown is banged and bent. She is embarrassed to wear her real hair in public, because she is convinced that she will be scrutinized for it. She begs God for something that will lift this burden. Then she buys something to wear over her hair to cope with this pain. She needs something to cover up her insecurity. She hides her crown and neglects its care. But while her hair is hidden, she feels a false sense of power that vanishes when natural elements can expose her. She covers her majesty by hiding her crown so that no one feels threatened by her power. Society, mothers or husbands falsely praise her because she looks like what they're used to.

Please, let her live! Let her discover herself in truth! Let her see her own reflection as *marvelous* in His sight! Encourage her choice to be free from false standards and expectations. Let our sister be who God created her to be. Express to her that she is gorgeous with or without the weaves, wigs or lye. It's not about the hair, but it's about what's inside. Help her to find her crown, shine it and place it back on her head where it belongs, for all to see. A crown is made for the person; a person is not made for the crown.

I made a vow to myself about myself. I vowed to never allow who I am and who God created me to be to become influenced by how others want to see me. I vowed that I would not be consumed by the standards of beauty in this society. I would not be consumed by other people's opinions, and I would not let them dampen my self-esteem. I vowed to let neither my hair nor my skin color make me feel less beautiful or less valuable. I vowed to let neither my hair nor my skin color place me on a pedestal above others. I vowed to let my hair and my skin color tell a story that will represent Someone bigger than me. I vowed to be an example for little girls all over the world, especially those little girls that look like me, who need a representation of what God-given strength looks like. I vowed to pursue my dreams despite all opposition. I vowed to celebrate others' God-given gifts. I vowed to sow seeds of hope and encouragement. I vowed to use my victories as a gateway to edify someone else. I vowed to not turn my hair into an idol.

Shrinkage is Not the Devil

The saying "feelin' yourself" is used in today's pop culture. I define "feelin' yourself" as the permission you give yourself to be arrogant about how you look or feel, based on something good that has happened in your life. You can say to somebody, "I see you are feelin' yourself today with the new car that you bought with your raise." Or you can say to others, "This new raise has me feelin' myself!" Side-note: I could be an editor for the Urban Dictionary. I feel like I am gifted in being able to articulate through writing slang and mottos from 2015 and beyond ...or maybe I'm just feelin' myself.

There was a day, yes *one day*, that I had an awesome hair day. My twist out was literally perfect. The correct definition-to-frizz ratio for the perfect hair volume was simply unreal. There was the proper amount of bounce which made my hair move when I walked or when I dramatically turned my head to face someone at the sound of my name. And when the wind blew, it brushed past my tresses so gently to make even my nape naps move left and right. Each strand was as perfectly coiled as those little springs that pop out of your mechanical pencil. I was *feelin' myself.* Throughout the day, I would take a small section of my hair and pull it down straight in order to project how long my hair would be if I were to straighten it. I smirked when the tip of my finger and the ends of my strands hit my collarbone. Progress! Eventually, this good hair day came to an end. As days passed, my scalp would itch—the indication that Wash Day was approaching. I spent that once-dreaded hour of washing and conditioning my hair with a newfound excitement and anticipation to check my length again. I loved seeing my wet coils brush the edge of my shoulders. I massaged in my leave-in conditioner and then stepped out of the shower. As I dried myself off, I noticed that my hair wasn't gently grazing anything anymore; I didn't feel it on my shoulders. I then stood before the mirror and behold: my nemesis and I met again. His name is Shrinkage. Shrinkage, commonly known as the devil himself, is what happens when your hair soaks up all the moisture it can and shrivels to eliminate all of the length you once displayed. The majority of naturalistas absolutely loathe Shrinkage because we feel it discredits all your progression of growth. Natural hair scholars have tried to deem Shrinkage as positive because actually, it is a sign of having healthy hair. I honestly don't care. I want my "swingage" when my hair is dry and wet, no exceptions.

As much as I hate Shrinkage, I have come to the realization that Shrinkage isn't the devil. Shrinkage is actually needed in your journey. For me, it is humbling. Shrinkage reminds me that I should be more worried about health than length. Without Shrinkage, I would be too consumed with the fact that my hair could swing, rather than it being able to retain moisture and keep its curl pattern. God allowed Shrinkage to show me what being humble and meek truly is. Meekness is when you have the power to impose your will, however you choose not to because it may not glorify God; meekness is submission to the Holy Spirit against your flesh. I could always keep my hair stretched out and in full swing effect, but I would clearly be "feelin' myself" too much to the point where I become prideful and superficial. I need Shrinkage for my own personal balance. I don't need to always show people that I've grown; as long as I am aware that I am spiritually healthy and my relationship is continuously growing with the Lord, I'm fine. In Matthew 6:5 it says, "And when you pray, you shall not be like the hypocrites. For they love to pray standing in the synagogues and on the corners of the streets, that they may be seen by men. Assuredly, I say to you they have their reward." I don't want my reward from men to be my priority. I just want my reward in Heaven from God. I now *own* my shrinkage and you should own your shrinkage, too. It is what makes and keeps you humble.

Wash Day is Like Sunday Service For Hair

Wash Day is the foundation of a good hair day. I know from experience that my style can't reach its full potential without proper grooming and training. I have to ultimately give my hair all the attention it needs to survive in harsh weather and/or manipulative hairstyles. Wash Day brings me so much joy even with its demand of responsibility. I can't wait to finally get home, decide on the products that I am going to use that day, and figure out my choice of hairstyles for the week. After a week of sticky product build up, itchy scalp, dry ends and a strong attempt to preserve my last style, I beg myself to reserve some time out of my busy schedule to give myself some tender love and care.

My Wash Day begins with detangling before I hop in the shower. I need to get my hair un-knotted and ready to receive proper care. If I step into the shower and shampoo right away without detangling, all the hidden knots and tangles will be a hindrance in retaining my length and force breakage. When detangling is complete, I can now enjoy my warm water and creamy shampoo combo-massage, which preps me for my soothing and smoothing deep conditioning. I can feel all of my worries about dry hair and massive shedding wash away as my curls shrink up into tight, springy coils. My scalp is cool, calm and has collected all of the moisture it retained from my choice of conditioner. I patiently let the mixture sit on my head and soak into each strand for the maximum benefit. When prompted, I rinse it off with cool water. If my hair agrees with the chosen conditioner, I can instantly feel the results as I touch my fluffy, light, cotton like fro. To top off my Wash Day duties, I apply my favorite leave-in conditioner and then proceed to style. I am confident and ready, knowing that the week ahead will be filled with good hair days.

There are moments when I don't feel like washing my hair. Yes, my scalp may itch a little, but for the most part I still have some definition left in my last twist out to carry me through a couple more days. I have product build up from the last styling gel I used, but I just don't *feel* like washing my hair. I convince myself that I can make it through with just a quick co-wash and wash and go, I'll be fine. I tell myself that whatever else I have to do that afternoon is more important than my upkeep and well-being. I throw myself off my own path to healthy hair by choosing to avoid the commitment of consistency and discipline. I'll pay for my neglect when I see the split ends and breakage that stunts my growth. You must shape a routine that works and has proven results, and you *must* stick to it. Nothing can replace Wash Day and all that it embodies.

Yes, Wash Day can be tedious, but it's worth it and oh-so necessary! Without Wash Day, your hair cannot reach its full potential. You need refreshment and revitalization after all that you placed your hair through during the week prior. After I have pulled on my hair all week from a high puff or stretching it at night to keep it from matting, or even after my hair has brushed and rubbed against my collar of mixed material, I need rejuvenation via my communion of conditioner.

Wash Day is like sweet Sunday service at church. When I have gone through tests and trials from life's woes throughout the week, I look forward to Sunday, my personal Wash Day, to be cleansed by the blood of Jesus. I can release all of my worries and cares from the week as I detangle my attitude and prepare myself to receive God's Word. I let the songbirds of music prepare my soul to receive the revelation, and the melodies from Heaven cleanse me from the nastiness of this world. I release my worship and repent from the dirt that I have accumulated in my mind, body and spirit. After my spirit is prepared through praise and worship, God's Word is imparted into my heart. I reflect on His Word, letting it marinate in all the places that need repair. God's Word washes me, leaving me soft, tender and humble to be molded into whatever the Lord sees fit. I "leave-in" the chosen scripture that I need to apply to my life, and get ready to "style" in this world from the anointing God has given me. I absolutely love Wash Day!

Nothing can substitute for a healthy, consistent church home that pours into you. You miss the pleasant conversation and edifying community when you just watch church on television or read a "quick" scripture at home. You miss the experience of worshipping before the Lord in His ordained and Holy temple. To be in the company of true family, witnesses of Christ, and the pouring out of the divine Holy

Spirit is unmatched. The witness of a powerful breakthrough of a brother or sister, the tears of joy and shout of triumph from a freed saint—it's all worth it. Find yourself the right shampoo, conditioner and leave-in that works for your hair, be consistent, and watch your hair grow. Find yourself a local church home with a pastor that teaches the Word and is consistent, and watch yourself grow.

When Deep Conditioning Conditions Your Soul

Deep conditioning is my favorite part of Wash Day. When I was younger and my mother did my hair, I hated, and I mean absolutely *hated*, deep conditioning. I spent what felt like hours sitting idly under a dryer with moist hair in a plastic shower cap, only to realize that this was just the halfway mark through Wash Day. I was really bothered that this process took so long that it made me despise deep conditioning. I didn't comprehend how beneficial deep conditioning was for my hair. I slowly but surely experienced the benefits of a good deep conditioner treatment when I felt the remarkable results in my hair afterward. When I saw the benefits, I wanted to continue to see the same results. Deep conditioning gave me and continues to provide me with strength, elasticity, moisture, repair and manageability. I had to put my patience in order and set aside time for this extra-necessary care.

Deep conditioning is an intimate time for textured hair. It's the only time that your hair can be marinated in essential ingredients for deep penetration in your scalp and hair shaft. Whether you schedule a sit-down under a hooded dryer or you improvise with a plastic grocery bag around your head for the clever green house effect or baggy method (the trapping of body heat from the compression of a plastic cap or bag around your head to lock in moisture and create elasticity), you are in the process of rejuvenation. After the allotted time has expired, you then rinse out the conditioner and proceed to the next steps of Wash Day. The Lord has shown me that the same intimacy you experience with your hair during a deep conditioning treatment is the same intimacy that you experience when you spend time with Him by reading His Word.

Bible study is a personal, devoted time that you must spend with God in order to receive the necessary care, attention, understanding and direction that you need in life. Whether this takes place in a group study, listening to an audiotape, or just curling up by yourself to read, digesting the Word of God reaps great benefits in your life. The Word of God gives you peace, wisdom, security, confirmation, deliverance, breakthrough and insight, just to name a few.

I'm going to be honest: I never really understood the importance reading the Bible on a daily basis. It took too long to read, I didn't quite understand everything I read and most days, I didn't feel like setting aside even 30 minutes of my time. Looking back, I could have been further along in my journey (the same with my natural hair journey) if I would have remained consistent and self-disciplined to make time to "deep condition." With any other subject or thing in life that I don't understand, I sought understanding and found it. When I couldn't seem to realize why my hair wasn't growing past my shoulders, I researched and found what I was doing wrong and changed my habits. When my life was in despair and confusion and heart break set in, I prayed about what I was doing wrong and after God told me the answer, I changed my habits. The answer given to me was that I wasn't deep conditioning on a consistent basis. I wasn't seeking the Lord with all of my heart through His Word daily, so I lacked what I needed to grow. Reading John 15:6-7, I'm reminded to abide in Christ. The scripture reads, "If anyone does not abide in Me, he is cast out as a branch and is withered; and they gather them and throw them into the fire, and they are burned. If you abide in Me, and My words abide in you, you will ask what you desire, and it shall be done for you." I learned my lesson: in order to continue to grow in my faith and relationship, I had to read His Word. If I wanted Christ to be with me, His Word had to be in me. God's Word is promise, wisdom, truth and life, if I rejected or neglected His Word, I'm rejecting and neglecting promise, wisdom, truth and life. I had made a conscious decision to make sure to make time to spend with my Father in Heaven. I'm reminded in Joshua 1:8-9, "This Book of the Law shall not depart from your mouth, but you shall meditate in it day and night, that you may observe to do according to all that is written in it. For then you will make your way prosperous, and then you will have good success." That sounds a lot like promise, wisdom, truth and life! It never fails that after you deep condition your hair, your strands feel softer, more moisturized and more revitalized than they did before. The same happens after you deep condition yourself in the Word. You feel convicted, joyful, stronger and wiser than you did before. Take deep conditioning seriously and let it penetrate deep down in your soul.

Hi, My Name is Janay and I am a Recovering Product Junkie

I enjoy buying hair products. Some would say I have a little problem with purchasing them. There was a time when, on average, I bought new hair products twice a month. I was always searching for new results. If a product could offer me better results, I was sold. Certain products would advertise that they could create more definition, add more moisture, build more volume... the list goes on and on. Yet, once tried, the products failed to deliver. Now, I purchase new hair products only when I need something specific that differs from what I already have.

The key ingredient that I find works best for my hair is *water.* Water to my hair is like water to a flower; without water, it dies. If a product had the correct ratio of water to natural ingredients in it, the more effective my results were. If a product contained just a small portion of water, I could tell, because my hair would be left sticky, soggy and clumpy. If the product contained things like polyethylene, sodium laureth sulfate, or isopropyl alcohol, I could also tell because my hair would be left dry, brittle and lifeless. However, a product made with the right amount of water leaves my hair shiny, defined and hydrated. My hair needs water.

Water for my hair is like the Holy Spirit for my soul—I need it to survive. My hair needs water to retain moisture so my strands will not break and my hair can be worked into whatever shape that I want it to. I need the Holy Spirit so that, instead of being broken and lifeless, I will be filled with direction as He shapes me into who He wants me to be. If a church or a leader does not possess this ingredient, then they're not for me. Romans 8:13-15 says that, "For if you live according to the flesh you will die; but if by the Spirit you put to death the deeds of the body, you will live. For as many as are led by the Spirit of God, these are the sons of God. For you did not receive the spirit of bondage again to fear, but you received the Spirit of adoption by whom we cry out, 'Abba, Father.'" If someone is elevated to a position to edify, encourage and teach the Bible, but the Holy Spirit is not present in their words, I can tell through discernment given to me from God. If a teacher of the Word is filled with pride, illicit motives or inaccuracy, then by the grace of God, I can tell. When someone teaches from the Word of God in submission to the Holy Spirit with proper knowledge, there is an instant confirmation in my heart and soul, which verifies that God is present and pleased. The Word stays with me and I can see results based on my acceptance and understanding of it. When I have found the right product, I stick with it and use it until I am led to use something else. If it is one of my staple products that have done wonders for my hair, I don't hesitate to share it with others. I only hope that I am living proof that the product works; I only hope that I am living proof that Jesus works.

I know when a product works for my hair because I see results. A lot of times, people recommend certain products for me to try that work for them. I listen to their witness and then I examine their hair. Is their hair in good standing? If not, I won't try the product they recommend. If their hair seems healthy, then I personally research the products they used and I contemplate a purchase. Sometimes the product has the amazing results, and sometimes my hair doesn't agree with the formula. The same is with hearing the Word of God from a pastor, evangelist, minister etc. Someone may recommend you to a place of worship to hear a word, but first and foremost, you must examine their example. We may not be perfect, but you can discern someone's heart and motives by their actions and their pursuit of Jesus. What fruit are they bearing? Matthew 7:15-16 says, "Beware of false prophets, who come to you in sheep's clothing, but inwardly they are ravenous wolves. You will know them by their fruits. Do men gather grapes from thorn bushes or figs from thistles?" Jesus said it best and said it first: actions speak louder than words. Observance of character can give you insight into the fruit that others bear. Words may sound great, but actions reveal greater—especially actions made after a mistake or wrongdoing. If you feel led, visit a friend's church home and examine for yourself if that is where you need to be planted in order to grow. Discern whether or not the Holy Spirit is present in the church. If something doesn't sit right with you—in your spirit and not your emotions—then ask God to lead you somewhere else. I jokingly call myself a product junkie because I am always striving to hear and understand the Word of God in different ways. I continuously research to find ministries that solely preach the Bible and not their own opinion. I say that I am a recovering product junkie because I am learning that every ministry isn't for me to receive from. My recovery is adhering to the right "product" through the discernment of the Holy Spirit. In Isaiah 30:21 it tells us, "Your ears shall hear a word behind you, saying, 'This is the way, walk in it,' Whenever you turn to the right hand or whenever you turn to the left." God has a way of leading us to the right place of worship where you can receive love, truth, growth and fellowship. He has the power and authority to usher us into the appropriate congregation and allow us to receive a message from the appropriate leader of the church. Always read the ingredients on the label and try the product out for yourself, if that is where God is leading you.

How I Got Punished With Heat Damage

Heat damage is when the temperature of a hair tool (like a flat iron) is placed at an extremely high heat, and if heat protectant isn't applied or if the heated tool is used too frequently, it damages the hair cuticles and ruins the natural curl pattern. The result of heat damage is limp, straightened strands, even when the hair is wet. Heat damage is noticeable when your strands will not revert back to their natural curly form. To get rid of heat damage, you must cut off the burnt and damaged strands.

I know for a fact that the Lord punished me with heat damage. He ultimately used heat damage as a lesson to teach and change me. Let me tell you the story:

I got impatient. You know, as a natural girl, you get that itch every once in a while to straighten your hair. You pull and stretch your hair periodically to see how much your hair has grown, just imagining the length it would be if it were flat ironed. I had that itch, and I had it bad.

My anxiety also came from the fact that I was restless in twisting my hair every five days. I was ready for the routine wrap and gentle comb-out in the mornings. Pulling my ends and checking the mirror every day, I thought to myself, "It's time to scratch this straightening itch!" I called my stylist and asked her if I could come in the next day. I couldn't wait. She was booked and said she could fit me in next week, which was more than 8 days away. I politely declined. I couldn't wait that long...I wanted "swingage!" So, of course, I took matters into my own hands. I washed, conditioned, deep conditioned and saturated every part of my head with the most potent heat protectant I had. I was ready, or so I thought. I grabbed my blow dryer, shook off the dust particles (I'm being dramatic, of course I wouldn't use a dusty hair tool on my hair), attached the comb and went to work. I didn't blow dry it too straight, but just to the point that a flat iron could pick up the rest of the work with minimal heat. I had watched many YouTube tutorials on straightening natural hair without getting heat damage. I just *knew* I would be okay.

I literally prayed as my flat iron was warming up, "Lord, please provide me with your grace and mercy and do not let me get heat damage. I know I can do this and it will not be a mess..." I then grabbed the flat iron, checked the heat thermostat to see it was still at 350 degrees, grabbed a small section of hair from the back of my head and made my first pass through. My hair obeyed the iron and laid flat on my shoulders. Everything seemed fine, so I continued section by section, only using one pass, *maybe* two. Then I began to notice something. As I advanced in my straightening, the first section I started with began to slowly but surely puff and frizz. The once-smooth pieces were now dusty looking and resembled the blown out hair I had before using the flat iron. I was irritated and growing impatient with how time consuming this had become, and I went back over all the puffy parts with another pass or two of heat. Finally, I was almost finished and just the front section was left. At the time, my hair wasn't long enough for my liking to incorporate a middle part, so I had to style the front of my head with the infamous middle school swoop bang. It didn't lay quite as flawlessly as I expected after one pass through, so I went ahead and pressed on my poor front bangs about 5 times. As I was doing this, the back of my head continued to swell up, so I proceeded to crack down on those parts too. I was determined to get all of my hair to lay flat with no residue of thickness. It didn't work. After I finished attempting to straighten my hair, I just stood in the mirror and looked back at my reflection. *What in the world is this? Why, Janay? Why? You should have just waited until there was an opening for an appointment, because you look like an 80's sitcom flashback.* It was a disaster. I grabbed my satin scarf and wrapped it up in hopes that my nighttime sleep would place pressure on my hair to make it lay flat. That didn't work. When I woke up, my hair actually looked *worse.* My length was gone due to my puffy ends and the accidental "wrap bump" which made me look like I could have been an extra in the movie *The Help.* I was thinking that I would NEVER straighten my hair again. It looked horrible. So, I placed a quick braid in the front to disguise my shameful bangs and let the puffy back of my hair just hang loose. I made the best out of my disapproved style. I bit the bullet and creatively styled my hair from what now looked like a regular blow out for the next three days. Finally, I was fed up. I couldn't take it any longer and had to wash my hair and revert it to its curly state. I hopped in the shower, rinsed, lathered and repeated with no worries—until I looked at myself in the mirror. With the leave-in conditioner sitting in my hair, a big chunk of straggly straight strands stared right back at me. They were hanging there lifeless and dead with the rest of my vibrant, bouncy curls questioning my loyalty. What did I do? I gave myself heat damage.

That itch of curiosity combined with my impatient zealousness to do things on my own was a recipe for disaster. I learned from my hair that in life, I must wait on God's approval first. Too many times I have gotten excited about something and completely jumped out on a limb before God equipped me to be successful. *It may be a **good** idea, but is it a **God** idea?* I ask that question to myself now when faced with anxiety about a decision. God revealed to me to begin a ministry that would include philanthropy. I heard him loud and clear, so I did it. I rushed and did all the paperwork for a Limited Liability Company only to find out that I was operating in the wrong season with the wrong mindset for this ministry. So I had to dissolve that LLC, and in the process I wasted so much money, time and effort. The ministry I now have been blessed with and assigned to, March 31st Ministries, was the vision God revealed to me then, but I was not suppose to execute it in that season; I was just suppose to plan. God revealed to me the vision, but He was still taking me through the process to prepare me for the victory. I thank God that I learned that lesson and have been prepared and groomed for victory through March 31st Ministries. I literally had to beat Philippians 4:6-7 into my head to learn to move when God tells me to move. It has become my personal mantra when I feel excited or over-zealous to do something without wisdom, direction or provision.

> *Janay, chill. Remember that the Lord told you to be anxious for absolutely nothing, and in everything you do, by prayer and supplication and thanking Him, you can make all of your requests known. You know He told you that once you make your entire request known, He will give you peace about everything you are anxious, worried or nervous about. Believe and trust your Father, In Jesus' Name.*

The Lord knows how hardheaded I am. When I want my way, He teaches me a lesson by letting me burn myself. I am disobedient sometimes, but I learn my lesson. His grace and mercy, however, is always present. The result of my impatience and moving before His timing isn't as bad as it should be. The heat damage that I could have caused to my hair when I straightened it myself wasn't as bad as it should have been. I could have had damage all over my head, but I now appreciate the small sections that I had to sacrifice in order to keep my hair healthy. I hate heat damage and I see my fault in it as well. Next time I straighten my hair, I will not be doing it myself, and I will wait until the time is right.

Trims are Necessary

Split, raggedy ends need to go;
Keep delaying that trim, and your hair won't
grow.

You fuss and you fight to keep them near,
Then you complain that your hair won't grow
past your ear.

I understand, you want to keep your length,
But what is the purpose, if the hair is brittle with
no strength?

When your hair is straight and your ends look
like straw,
A stylist can't let you leave without a trim, it's
their law.

Let them get the shears out and snip, snip that
hay,
But remember, stylist, a trim is a trim, don't get
carried away.

Some trim once, twice, even three times a year,
And that, ladies, is how growth will appear.

You see, trims are needed every once in a while,
Get rid of the damage for a better lifestyle.

The ends of your hair are the oldest part as well,
Some people who have been around the longest
can no longer dwell.

Wish them a goodbye, and tell them that you're
through,
Realize that letting them go is the best decision,
for the both of you.

Those raggedy ends may have seemed to be fine,
But if you look in the mirror you would see; they
were blocking your shine.

Sometimes weak ends are spotted easily and can
be cut off just like that,
Or sometimes heat, pressure and straightening
is needed to expose the rat.

Yes, we are still talking about split ends, just
wanted to flip the script,

Or has this poem shifted, and now we are
discussing an un-ordained relationship?

Don't let people, places or things that hinder
your spiritual growth stay in your life,
Because, just like split ends, they will cause you
great strife.

Either way you look at it, there is an expiration
date for everything,
Wait, I lied, there isn't an expiration date on our
time in Heaven, with Jesus the King.

Why I Have a Love-Hate Relationship With YouTube Hair Tutorials

I have a weird love-hate relationship with YouTube hair videos. Even though they are very informative, I don't really care for them. I can spend hours watching hair tutorial videos created and uploaded by other naturalistas. I search my desired hairstyle or topic that I want to watch and wait for the numerous options of videos and channels to appear. As I scroll, I try to find the most appealing video based on the thumbnail, and I want it within 8 minutes or less. I click on the best one and begin to take mental notes on every little detail the vlogger is performing. I get so inspired by the finished product, displayed with a unique editing extravaganza. Then it's my turn. I now have the desire to do exactly what the hair guru did, and I want the exact same results that she got. I roll out all of my hair products, even occasionally purchasing the products they recommended. As

I keep my phone nearby to replay their instructions, I believe that I am going to achieve the same, perfect results as the video I just watched.

The first time I tried to do a flexi rod set by myself with the guidance of a YouTube tutorial was very interesting. The young lady whose video I watched had the same hair texture as mine, but her hair was a little bit longer. I duplicated the exact brand of products, purchased the same color of flexi rod packs and mimicked every twisting wrist motion that she did. I let my hair dry overnight as the video instructed and applied the same "Take Down" method as she showed me in the video. My results were the complete opposite of hers! I didn't come close, at all, to her resemblance. I was disappointed again by my natural hair and its failure to deliver on the promise of versatility. However, I didn't give up. I tried the tips and tricks of other natural hair experts on different hairstyles like bantu knots, flat twist outs, finger coils and so many more, only to find myself with the same unfavorable results. I decided that if my hair didn't look like theirs, I was never going to try another YouTube tutorial again. This changed when I surprised myself by finding my own hairstyling techniques.

I was watching a hair tutorial about a braid-out, which is a hairstyle that uses dried, unraveled braids to create a curl pattern on natural hair. The vlogger had gone through each step to demonstrate how she achieved her full, bouncy curls. She had great results, so I decided that I would continue watching. As she demonstrated her instructions, I disagreed with a small portion of what worked for her based on my own experiences. I knew that I couldn't use certain products that she used or even apply the products in the order in which she did. I took the information that I needed from her video and decided to combine it with my own steps that would work best for me. I used products that I liked and braided my hair the best way I knew how. I let my hair dry overnight, and in the morning crossed my fingers in hopes of accomplishing a style worth wearing. As I slowly unraveled my braids, I could already see the consistent definition in each section. I couldn't hide the smile on my face, and I felt relieved that my time was not wasted again from a new hairstyle fail. This time around, I achieved the look I desired, and my results looked even better than that of the tutorial video. God showed me right there in that moment that all I had to do was be myself. It's okay to follow others' suggestions, but do not lose yourself in the process.

We can all arrive to a place of victory, but that doesn't mean we take the same route to get there. The Lord has blessed each of us with our own special instructions and gifts for what He wants us to accomplish in our lives. My instructions to achieve what God has called me to do, may not be the same as yours. That's one of the beauties of having natural hair; no two people's hair are exactly alike. This is another beauty of being a Christian; no two people's callings are exactly alike. The Lord convicted me heavily to be content and trust in His divine plan for me, instead of trying to be like someone else. Each of us has our own special ministry, whether we think we are worthy or not. With the same concept as in the chapter *Fro Envy*, do not covet another's ministry, but instead celebrate them and be proud to be yourself in your ministry. Your style of preaching, teaching, evangelizing, leading, speaking, thinking, parenting, creating, coaching, painting, acting, singing, assisting, writing or whatever else, is to the glory of God.

Someone is dependent on *you* and your unique style to strengthen their relationship with Christ. Someone is depending on your talents to help them understand the Kingdom of God. Just like following YouTube tutorials, you get the best results when you are *yourself* and not anyone else.

Chicks With the Kinks Still Get the Winks

All my ladies gather around. I have a story to tell. Well, more like a little motivational chat. As an African American woman, do you have moments when you feel powerless in a world that seems to be ran by egotistical men? As a black woman in this world, do you feel as though you have to go above and beyond just to be considered or included at the standard level? Our society is built to make us feel like we do not belong, judging based on the number of items, ideas and places that don't cater to the desires of black women, yet cater to every other race and gender. We attempt to buy jeans and they don't correctly fit our curvy hips and thick thighs. We turn on the television to find just a handful of colored representation in movies and TV shows, when we make up a great proportion of the population. We are just discovering our own special aisle when buying hair products because hair companies have finally realized that not all hair is blonde or brunette, straight and fine. We got tired of not finding anything that works and started making our own products. Our workplace has told us that our hair doesn't belong, especially if styled to represent pride in our culture, whether having braids or locs. Our work ethic is questioned when we decide to wear our hair in a style that resembles our history. They encourage us to wear hair that emulates the texture of the majority. Whether it is your boss, your undiversified place of employment, your church, your school or the media, this world is full of people with unequal standards and biases. It can have us brown-skinned ladies feeling dominated to the point where we may question our significance. This friction can cause us to act out of character by suppressing our emotions or exerting them, because we get frustrated and overwhelmed with the obvious disrespect from society (and the disrespect from our own people, as well).

We're in a constant battle, either avoiding or submitting to the "Angry Black Woman" stereotype when we get fed up. We are strong, feisty and speak our minds, but we don't always want to feel like we have to be. From the illusion that our male African American counterparts are not holding their end of the bargain, we may feel alone and unsupported in this million-man march. The illusion is false representation that the majority of black men do not protect us black women, by standing up for us on our behalf. The illusion is false representation that the majority of black men do not take care of their children and are dead-beat dads. The illusion is false representation that the majority of black men, or "successful" black men, do not desire to be married to black women. The illusion is false representation that the majority of black men kill each other and grow up in poor ghettos and only strive to be dope dealers, murderers, weed smokers, rappers or professional basketball or football players. The illusion is false representation that the majority of black men do not attend church or know God intimately, because we personally do not *see* them where we may attend church. The illusion is a trick and a lie from the devil himself to breed discouragement, divisiveness, disgrace and hopelessness to our culture and our women. Statistics don't lie, but liars surely use and skew statistics. Our mind has played tricks on us, making us think that we need to pick up the slack and be the man *and* woman of the house.

Sometimes the pain of disappointment has pushed us into doing this by ourselves without asking for help, even when we truly wish we had plenty. We look around and the illusion makes us believe that we are the overpopulated and unappreciated breed of women; the devil is a liar! We think we outnumber our colored brothers greatly because the illusion states that they all died young, are not financially stable, are incarcerated or are living a lifestyle filled with sin without repentance. Despite it all, we are successful, but something always seems to be missing: our womanhood. How do we battle this conundrum and keep our identity as sweet, yet strong Christian woman?

We must recognize our power in Jesus Christ. We as women have more power than we think. I know this might seem like known information, but maybe we haven't fully grasped the concept of how strong our influence is. God has embedded within us with certain natural gifts that only a woman can possess. He gave us special discernment, known as female intuition. He has given us the power of influence and the ability to multiply, amongst many other things. The choice is ultimately up to *us* to decide if we are going to be virtuous women of

God with morals and standards for His Kingdom or women that can bring pain to many, under the influence of the devil from a series of ungodly decisions. God strengthens women to be helpers, encouragers, managers of the home, businesswomen, creators, teachers, nurturers, forgivers, lenders, prayer warriors and healers (Proverbs 3:10-31), just to name a few great characteristics of God's ideal woman. The devil likes it when we are under his influences by displaying behaviors of deceit, falsehood, insecurity, scandal, gossip, laziness, jealously, envy, confusion and promiscuity. We sell ourselves short when we dumb down to the level of the devil. Our influence is so great that we can be used in steering the direction of the future for our family and loved ones under the authority of the Holy Spirit, by obeying God's magnificent Word. We conquer our conundrum and solidify our identity in this world by utilizing the gifts we've been given for the glory of God.

How do I know that God created women with great capabilities and purpose? Because the purpose that God placed in us to fulfill can be accomplished in the absence of a man. We as women are so powerful that our fulfillment of our purpose on earth does not require a man to accomplish it; the only man we truly *need* is Jesus Christ himself. We are receivers and multipliers; we can create life in more than one way. I love the notion and saying, "Whatever you give a woman, she multiplies." This is true, we are multipliers. A man gives us his seed and we can create children; if you give us groceries, we can create a meal; and if you give a woman grief, we have been known to create nightmares. Even in our anatomy and the way God created us, women are receivers and creators while men are givers and providers. We receive and produce greatness. We can influence a goal for accomplishment or hinder a goal in abortion. The more we continue to refine ourselves in Christ, the more influence we have over our culture. When we say "No! Stay away!" and *refuse* to accept less than what we deserve and what the Lord has for us in all areas of our lives, the entire "game" changes and standards are raised.

Please be encouraged that there are great men of God out in this world. Don't let what you do not *see* influence your hope for the future and discourage your growth in this season. Godly men feel as though there are no godly women left in this world too, and we all know that is incorrect. Let God continue to strengthen us and refine us before He introduces us to each other; that's a match-made in Heaven. Don't get caught up in the hype of the illusion and lose your identity in Christ. I had to change my perspective and see things the way that God sees them. If we are constantly reading, watching and listening to worldly media, of course our outlook on ourselves, life and men will be negatively influenced and will counter what God believes. If we are indulging in poor television shows, listening to degrading music and reading biased, untrue propaganda that portray African Americans in a bad image, then of course we will start to believe everything certain media outlets display. We have to change our perspective and give our attention to things that edify, such as positive television shows on one accord with God's agenda, inspiring music with a meaningful message, and pure, powerful reading material, such as the Bible. When I began to retrain and reprogram my way of thinking into the way that Christ wanted to me think, then my perception of myself and others began to shift and my hope was restored. Romans 12:2 calls us to renew our minds. It reads, "And do not be conformed to this world, but be transformed by the renewing of your mind, that you may prove what is that good and acceptable and perfect will of God."

As I've been renewing my mind, I no longer take offense towards a society that doesn't meet my needs. Jesus takes good care of me and my cup runneth over. It doesn't bother me anymore that my hairstyles seemed to confuse my co-workers and I didn't fit in. I like my hair, and I know who I am in Christ. I don't rely on a mass representation of people that look like me or celebrate my culture in Hollywood, because the Lord has blessed me with amazing brothers and sisters I know personally who will represent my culture and get all the recognition, encouragement and praise that they deserve in their chosen endeavors. I like when I have to go above and beyond for borderline basic things to even be considered, because I realize that God is equipping me with extra wisdom needed to be phenomenal. I am reassured when I can't find the right pair of jeans or clothes that fit me just right because I like feeling unique and exclusive. Only the finest fabrics can cater to my beautiful body. I pray and mourn for our brothers who are incarcerated in a corrupt justice system, living in darkness because of sin, have passed away or can't get their financials situated, but I have hope for our future and I know God made someone especially for me that will exceed all of my expectations. I refuse to let this lost and dying world influence me to become anything opposing the powerful woman that God created me to be. I refuse to let this world display the illusion of a desolate land and that God's promises will not come to pass. Numbers 23:19 says, "God is not a man, that he should lie; neither the son of man, that he should repent: hath he said, and shall he not do it? Or hath he spoken, and shall he not make it good?" When we focus on Him instead of the problems and mishaps of this world and when we focus on us being extraordinary creatures in Christ, He showed me and I pray He shows you that, chicks with the kinks, *still* and always will, get the winks.

You are Your Hair

I know by this chapter title, I am defying everything that goes against the love myself anthem *I Am Not My Hair* by India Arie, but there is a purpose. I agree with the notion that our hair does not define us. However, your hair *is* a representation of who you are. First impressions are not everlasting, but first impressions are a quick glimpse of who you are and what you represent. Based on first impressions, our hair can reflect our personality, well-being and hygiene. Based on who we are and what we represent, we can influence people to get to know us or turn people off. Let's be real, the perception of the way I upkeep my natural hair can either influence them to return natural or completely turn them off from natural hair. I am a representation of natural hair, and if you are natural, so are you, even if you never asked for the responsibility. What about if you are not natural? If you aren't natural, the way you keep your relaxed hair or weave is a reflection of that style, your hygiene and personality too. When you think about it, it's kind of silly that people would stereotype a group based on how a handful of people act. But that is life. Based on the experience that we have with one person, we associate that experience with the entire group of people who share their traits. Sometimes, we are so displeased with our experience that there is no room for a second chance to change the opinion someone has already made.

The first time I saw a person with dreadlocks in their hair, I didn't like them (I will refer to dread locks as locs from this point on, in my opinion, there is nothing dreadful about them). The person whom I saw didn't keep their locs "kept" enough for my liking. It was my first time seeing them and it seemed like that's the only way I saw them from then on. As I got older, I just couldn't stand the sight of locs, which changed as I matured. I met a young lady in college that had the most gorgeous hair ever; her hair was loc'ed. Her hair looked healthy, well-kept and she reminded me of a modern-day hazelnut Rapunzel. My friends and I would ask her questions about her hair all the time and she educated me and changed my whole perspective of locs. From that point on, I asked more people with loc'ed hair about their experience with locs to the point, I respected and understood their choice of style. This isn't to say that I would choose this hairstyle (even though I have pondered on the idea more than once) but I respect and understand it. I have met plenty of people who were somewhat intrigued by my hair and I do not hesitate to explain to them why I returned natural and the hard work that goes into the upkeep. Many people have shared with me that they now have a better understanding of what being natural is, and might even try it. On the contrary, I have also neglected my hair and have been a poor representation of what natural hair is supposed to represent. There were days where I skipped Wash Day for the week, didn't deep condition, didn't detangle and just fixed my hair in an "I don't care" style and walked out the door. My representation was a mess. Sometimes, I just wish people would understand the movement and focus on that, instead of basing the entire movement on one natural woman. However, I might be the only representation that they ever encounter from the natural hair community, so I have to be the best representation I can be.

God showed me how representation of my hair related to representation of my relationship with Him. How I portray myself as a pronounced Christian is a reflection of God. I might be the only encounter someone may have with a believer, and what I am displaying paints a picture of the God I serve. Am I loving like Jesus? Am I controlling my mouth and temper? Am I speaking kind words to those that I know do not like me? Am I forgiving others like Jesus? Am I living a life that is full of repentance? Am I spreading the bountiful mercy of God on my life? I feel like I am always under the microscope. I pray people would experience Jesus for themselves and know that He is the only measuring stick to how Christians should act, but the reality is, not everyone does. Matthew 5:13 says, "You are the salt of the earth; but if the salt loses its flavor, how shall it be seasoned? It is then good for nothing but to be thrown out and trampled underfoot by men." We are called to be the salt to this earth; we are called to season love on all and spread His Word in truth. I must be used as a living example to display the transformative power of Jesus Christ. I care so much about the God I serve that I don't want any of my actions to misrepresent Him in any way. I am not perfect, but I hope people see His grace, favor and forgiveness all over me. This is why I say that I am my hair. My hair tells a story. My hair tells a story of who I am as a believer and my journey with Jesus Christ thus far. The Bible tells us in 1 Corinthians 11:15 that if a woman has long hair it is a glory for her, for her hair is given for a covering. My hair is my glory because it is my covering and my shield of security in knowing Whose I am. My hair is my glory because it represents transitioning my life back to Christ. My hair symbolizes the loving conviction and guidance from the Holy Spirit. My hair represents repentance. God has shown me how my hair represents character and growth spiritually and reflects His grace naturally. I am my hair because of the life that it represents, testifying to the glory of God. My hair is my testimony. My hair honors Jesus—not myself. Understand my story and know that your hair may tell a story as well.

God, Do You Like My Fro?

Father, you know that I love talking to
you and asking you for your
wisdom,

but there has always been this one thing
on my mind to ask you that I never
did, because I was worried about
the outcome.

You sent laborers to speak life into me, to
confirm all that I could be,

but within that prophecy, did you
envision this fro being a part of
me?

So I ask you this question, God: Do you
like my fro?

Is your hair like sheep's wool, is it
anything like mine?

Because the pictures and paintings of
Jesus with straight hair and blue
eyes are deceiving and they
changed the way beauty is defined.

You said in your pure Word that I was
made in Your image, which is Your
likeness,

but everywhere I turn I am told to blend
in with the darkness.

"Keep your hair straightened," they say,
"We have evolved from those
kinky naps."

Then, I stare deep into their eyes and see
the fear in their heart from a past
relapse.

This hair, this blessing, somehow reminds
them of the curse,

the guilt they now feel for their
treatment of us, or the pain of
slavery we felt when life was
perverse.

We used to be told to hide our unruly
hair, tie it down, so that it couldn't
be seen until we were home,

but oh, the day we rejoiced, at the
invention of the hot comb.

Now we can *surely* fit in, now they can
surely see that we belong,

showing off our press and curl for
approval, while they *still* label us
wrong.

So, Lord, I ask you again: Do you even like
my fro?

This past problem on my head, when my
ancestors were called negro.

Why would you give me this troubled
mane that society won't accept?

Why do they keep telling me that my hair
is "un-kept?"

I ask *You* in Heaven, because *You* are King
of all and *You* are the One.

I don't need anyone else's opinion,
biasness or concern; *You* are
Whom I want approval from.

My heart cries out to You, Lord. I need to
hear from You. I won't leave or go.

What is it that You, my Father, have to
say about my fro?

Then it happened, as I was on my knees, I
felt His Holy Spirit descend,

I began to cry and pour out my heart,
begging for Him to step in.

He always shows up when I call Him. He
knows just when to intervene,

"Go back to what you already know.
Psalms 139, verse fourteen."

I then told God, that I understood that
verse but everything around me
has my head in a cloud-

And before I could finish He cut me off: "I
didn't ask you about everything
around you. Go back to Psalms
139, verse fourteen and *read. it. out.
loud.*"

I humbled myself and submitted to His
Holy Spirit that I was among,

I obeyed His instructions as His precious
Words rolled off of my tongue.

"I will praise You, for I am fearfully and
wonderfully made; Marvelous are
Your works, and that my soul
knows very well."

He said, "Janay, My beautiful daughter, I
gave you and others alike that
kinky, curly, coily hair, because
you all have a story to tell.

I made everyone in this world in My
image, but to your kind, I knew
that My Holy Spirit would be
welcomed again to worship as one,

So My gift to you, I gave you the same
texture as Jesus My Son.

I gave gifts to My children of all shades,
for the Kingdom needs all for the
saving of lost souls,

So whatever it is that I blessed you with,
remember the reason for it and
play your role.

Don't get distracted by the enemy and
remember that my works are
marvelous,

walk in the purpose that I gave you and
bind those spirits of insecurity,
doubt and fearfulness.

Again, I told you before, I will *not* lie,

Again, I told you before, the God that I am
will *never* die.

So, I answered your question but I will say
it again: Daughter, I love your fro,

but I never created it for your glory; but
for *Mine* to grow."

About the Author

Janay Brinkley is founder and CEO of March 31st Ministries LLC and creator of JanayBrinkley.com, a God-led vision assigned to her, to spread the true and living word of God in compelling, relevant and inventive ways in order to usher effective growth, challenging change and empowering edification in Christ Jesus. As a former Division 1 Athlete, Graduate Student, Professional in Sports, Community Leader and Youth Advocate/Mentor, her passion is to edify and encourage others for the advancement of God's Kingdom here on earth. Janay is a native of Maryland and strives to always reveal God's revelation while being relevant and transparent in order to reach those around her.

Made in the USA
Lexington, KY
26 June 2017